I0762668

Little Mitchie

HOLIDAY BITES

FUN FOOD FOR EVERY SEASON

KIDS IN THE KITCHEN

Joanne Mattern

CREATING YOUNG NONFICTION READERS

Little Mitchie books spark curiosity and support early nonfiction reading for students in Grades 2-3. Designed to build vocabulary, support second language learners, and prepare readers for middle-grade content, each book includes helpful tips for parents and educators to build confidence and deepen understanding of the world.

TIPS FOR READING NONFICTION WITH BEGINNING READERS

Talk about Nonfiction

Begin by explaining that nonfiction books give us information that is true. The book will be organized around a specific topic or idea, and we may learn new facts through reading.

Look at the Parts

Most nonfiction books have helpful features. Our *Little Mitchie* titles include color photographs and graphic aids, a table of contents, a glossary, and an index. Share the purpose of these features with your reader.

Color Photos and Graphic Aids

A lot of information can be found by "reading" photos, charts, maps, and other graphic aids found within nonfiction texts. Help your reader learn more about the different ways information can be displayed.

Table of Contents

Located at the front of the book, this list shows the big ideas within the text and the page numbers where they can be found.

Glossary

Located at the back of the book, the glossary defines key words and phrases that are related to the topic. These words and phrases can be found in the text in colored type.

Index

Located at the back of the book, an index is an alphabetical list of topics and the page numbers where they can be found.

With a little help and guidance about reading nonfiction, you can feel good about introducing a young reader to the world of *Little Mitchie* nonfiction books.

Little Mitchie is an imprint of:

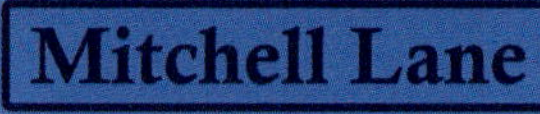

2001 SW 31st Avenue
Hallandale, FL 33009
mitchelllanepub.com

First Edition, 2027.

Author: Joanne Mattern
Designer: Bobbie Houser
Editor: Madison Greve

Library of Congress Cataloging-in-Publication Data
Title: Holiday Bites: Fun Food for Every Season / by Joanne Mattern

Description: Hallandale, FL : Mitchell Lane Publishers, [2027]

Identifiers:
ISBN 979-8-89260-927-2 (library bound)
ISBN 979-8-90145-013-0 (eBook)

Library of Congress Control Number: 2026936386

PHOTO CREDITS
Shutterstock: JeniFoto, cover, 1, 15; Taras Grebinets, 4; Viktoriia Ablohina, 5; Elena Veselova, 7; New Africa, 9; irina2511, 11; Pixel-Shot, 13; ZM.kichi, 17; JlynnBlev, 19; Lori Barbely, 21.

TABLE OF CONTENTS

HOW TO USE THIS BOOK

The kitchen is a great place to have fun! This book will help you make some delicious recipes.

Read each recipe first. Be sure to have everything you need in place before you start. Check that no one is **allergic** to any of the ingredients.

Wash your hands before you start.

Have an adult close by. Let them use knives and the stove.

Now, get ready to cook up some fun!

CONVERSION CHART

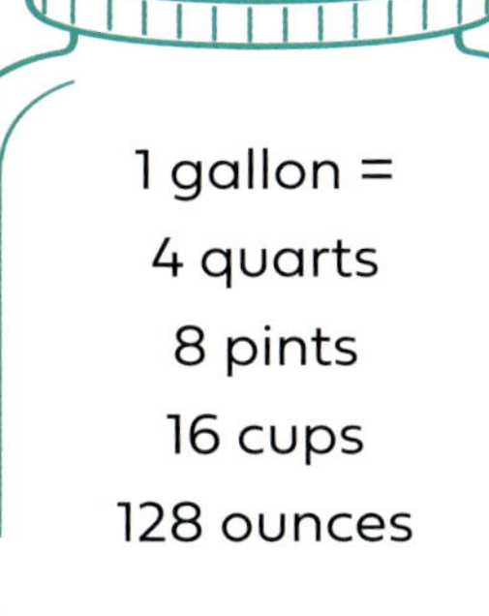

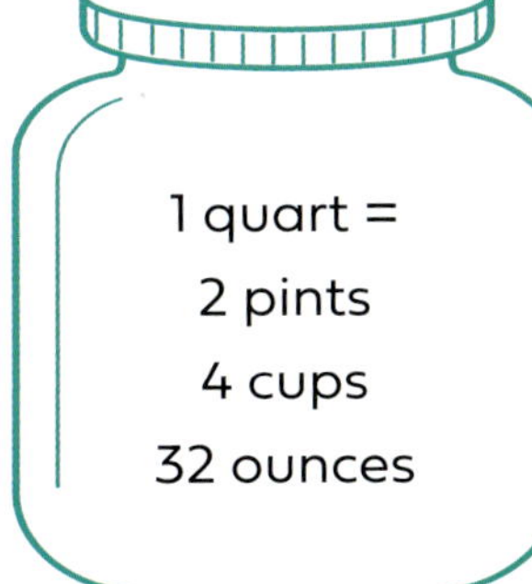

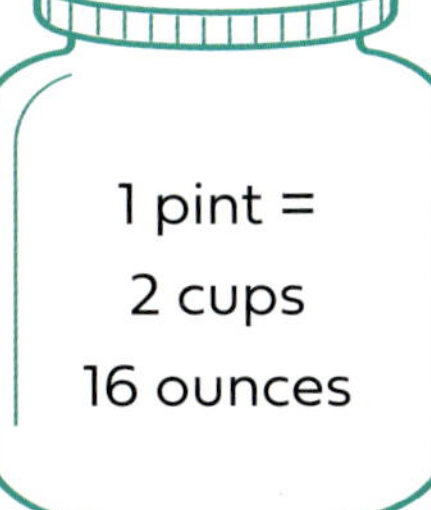

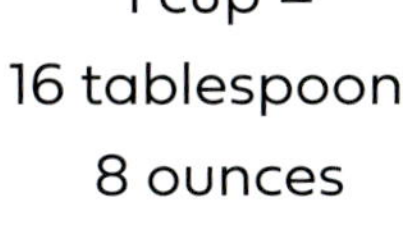
1 cup =
16 tablespoons
8 ounces

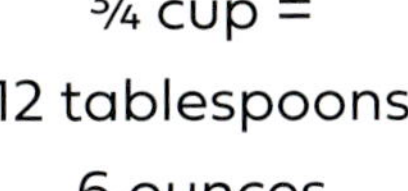
¾ cup =
12 tablespoons
6 ounces

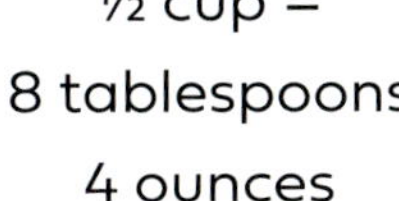
½ cup =
8 tablespoons
4 ounces

⅓ cup =
5 ⅓ tablespoons
2 ⅔ ounces

¼ cup =
4 tablespoons
2 ounces

3 teaspoons = 1 tablespoon (½ ounce)
2 tablespoons = ⅛ cup (1 ounce)
4 tablespoons = ¼ cup (2 ounces)
5 ⅓ tablespoons = ⅓ cup (2 ⅔ ounces)
8 tablespoons = ½ cup (4 ounces)
12 tablespoons = ¾ cup (6 ounces)
32 tablespoons = 2 cups (16 ounces)

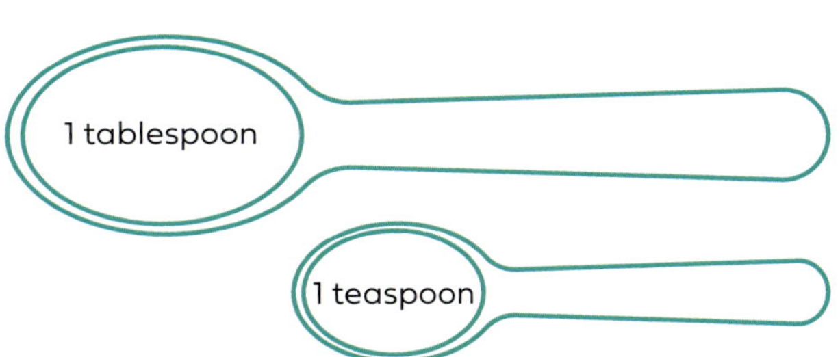

Chapter 1

NO-BAKE VALENTINE'S DAY COOKIES

Daniel carried his tray of Valentine's Day cookies into the classroom. "My dad helped me make these for the party!" he told everyone. "They taste so good!"

"They look delicious!" his teacher said with a smile. "I'm sure the class will really enjoy them."

Daniel passed out a treat to every classmate. His friends liked the cookies very much!

"They were fun to make," Daniel said as he shared the cookies with his friends. "I am glad you like them!"

You will need:

1 cup of crushed graham crackers

⅓-cup honey

1 teaspoon vanilla extract

A dash of salt

½-cup mini chocolate chips

Red, pink, and white sprinkles

½-cup peanut butter or nut butter

ALLERGY ALERT!

Directions:

Mix all the ingredients except the sprinkles together in a large bowl to make the **dough**.

Line a cookie sheet with **parchment paper**.

Pour the sprinkles in a small bowl.

Roll the dough into small balls.

Roll the balls in the sprinkles to cover them.

Place the balls on the cookie sheet. Place the sheet in the refrigerator overnight.

FUN FOOD FACT!
Candy is the most popular Valentine's Day gift.

Chapter 2

EASTER BIRD NESTS

"The treats you made look so pretty," Charlotte's cousin told her. "Thank you for bringing them to our Easter dinner."

"You're welcome," Charlotte said. "My mother found the recipe in an old cookbook. She said she used to make them with Grandmother, so we decided to make them together."

"Were they easy to make?" her cousin asked.

"Yes," Charlotte answered, "and fun too . . . I can't wait to share them with everyone!"

You will need:

1 package of vanilla Oreo™ cookies

4-ounce bar of cream cheese

1 cup chocolate chips

8-ounce bag of candy eggs

1 bag of coconut **flakes**

Directions:

Place the Oreo™ cookies in a **food processor**. With the help of an adult, **pulse** until the cookies are crushed into bits.

Mix the cream cheese and Oreo™ crumbs together in a large bowl and roll the mixture into balls.

Cover a plate with coconut flakes and gently roll each ball in the coconut until covered.

Place the balls on a cookie sheet lined with parchment paper.

Use the back of a scoop or small spoon to make a round **hollow** in each ball. Now you have nests!

Chill the dough in the refrigerator for 30 minutes.

With an adult's help, microwave the chocolate chips until they are completely melted.

Scoop the melted chocolate into the hollows in the nests.

Place 2 or 3 candy eggs in each nest.

Chill for 15 minutes.

Chapter 3

Turkey Pretzel Treats

"I love Thanksgiving," Chloe said to her Aunt Laura. "It's so fun to share a meal with the family."

"I have an idea. Let's make a special dessert," Aunt Laura said. "These treats are sure to make everyone feel thankful!"

Chloe had a good time cooking with Aunt Laura. “I’ve never seen treats like this,” Chloe said when they had finished. “They are fun to look at, and they will be fun to eat too!”

You will need:

12 large pretzel sticks

1 package of candy eyes

1 package of candy corn

2 cups chocolate chips

2 cups brown sprinkles

Directions:

Pour the sprinkles on a small plate and cover a tray with parchment paper.

Pour the chocolate chips in a small bowl. With an adult's help, microwave them until they melt.

Dip a pretzel stick halfway into the melted chocolate. Then roll it in the plate of sprinkles before setting it on the parchment paper.

Before the chocolate cools, stick 2 candy eyes near the top of the pretzel. Then add a piece of candy corn below so it sticks out like a turkey's beak.

Add 6–8 pieces of candy corn around the top of the pretzel to make the turkey's tail feathers.

Repeat these steps until you have a plate of turkey pretzels!

FUN FOOD FACT!

No one ate turkey at the first Thanksgiving! Instead, they feasted on deer meat, oysters, lobsters, and pumpkins!

Chapter 4

NEW YEAR'S PARTY ANIMAL DIP

George was up late on New Year's Eve. "What's for dessert?" he asked his mother.

"Party animals!" his mom said.

"I don't see any animals in here," George said. "That's silly."

"These animals are fun enough to eat," his mother said. "Take a look."

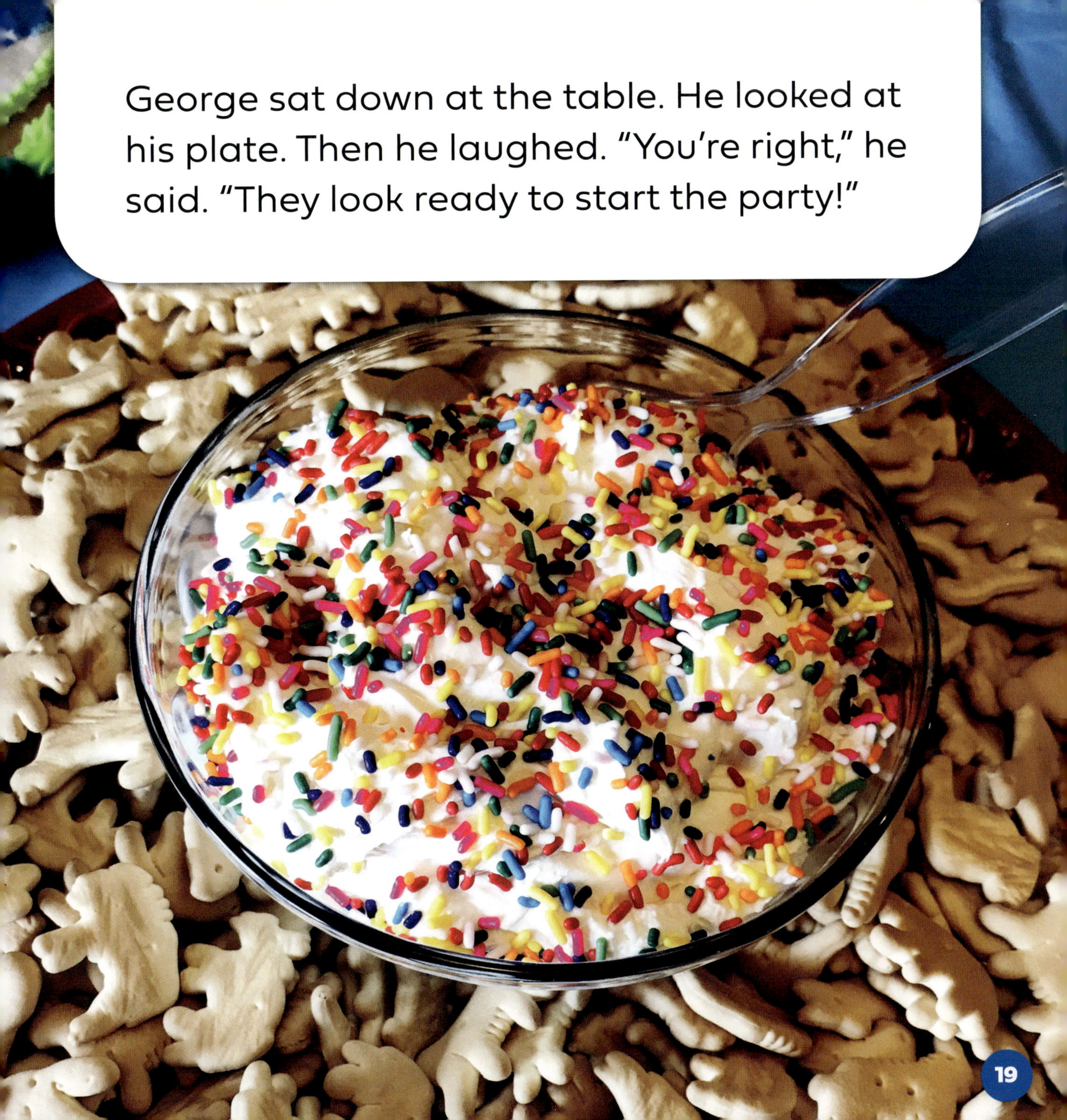

George sat down at the table. He looked at his plate. Then he laughed. "You're right," he said. "They look ready to start the party!"

You will need:

1 large box of animal crackers

1 box of birthday cake mix

1 small container of Cool Whip™

1 small container of vanilla yogurt

Rainbow sprinkles

Directions:

In a large bowl, add the Cool Whip™, birthday cake mix, and vanilla yogurt.

Add as many sprinkles as you want. Mix all the ingredients together to make the party dip.

Move the mixture to a medium bowl. Place the bowl in the middle of a large plate.

Top the dip with more sprinkles—as many as you want!

Pour the animal crackers out onto the plate so they go all the way around the bowl of dip.

FUN FOOD FACT!
A box of animal crackers can be used as a Christmas ornament! People used to hang the boxes on their trees using the string on the top of the box.

GLOSSARY

allergic (uh-LER-jik)—having a bad reaction to a food

dough (DOH)—a thick mixture of flour, liquids, or other ingredients

flakes (FLAYKS)—small, flat pieces

food processor (FOOD PRAH-sess-or)—a machine with spinning blades that can cut or blend foods

hollow (HAH-loh)—a small, round, sunken place

oysters (OI-sturz)—small sea animals with soft bodies that may be eaten and shells that open and close

parchment paper (PARCH-muhnt PAY-per)—a special sheet of paper that does not burn and keeps food from sticking

pulse (PULSS)—a setting on a food processor that works in short bursts

Further Reading

Imperial, Pia. *Cookies for Santa.* Grosset & Dunlap, 2023.

Richardson, Kristy. *Kid Chef Bakes.* Rockridge Press, 2020.

On the Internet

"Easy Holiday Treats to Make with Kids." PDX Parent.com
https://pdxparent.com/easy-holiday-treats-to-make-with-kids/
The short article has healthy, fruit-based snacks for the winter holidays.

"25 Holiday Recipes to Make with Kids." Weelicioius.com
https://weelicious.com/holiday-recipes-to-make-with-kids/
This article has many different holiday ideas for kids and parents to make together.

INDEX

ABOUT THE AUTHOR

Joanne Mattern loves snacking and eating fun food! She has written many nonfiction books for children, including cookbooks and books about holidays. Joanne lives in New York State with her family.